To Nancy
from May

I thought you would
love this book!

THE RED BOOK OF DOGS

THE RED BOOK OF DOGS

HOUNDS · TERRIERS · TOYS

JULIE MUSZYNSKI

COLLINS|DESIGN

An Imprint of HarperCollinsPublishers

THE RED BOOK OF DOGS
HOUNDS • TERRIERS • TOYS

HarperCollins books may be purchased for educational,
business, or sales promotional use. For information,
please write: Special Markets Department,
HarperCollins *Publishers*, 10 East 53rd Street, New York, NY 10022.

First Edition

First published in 2007 by:
Collins Design
An Imprint of HarperCollins*Publishers*
10 East 53rd Street
New York, NY 10022
Tel: (212) 207-7000
Fax: (212) 207-7654
collinsdesign@harpercollins.com
www.harpercollins.com

Distributed throughout the world by:
HarperCollins*Publishers*
10 East 53rd Street
New York, NY 10022
Fax: (212) 207-7654

Design: Agnieszka Stachowicz

Library of Congress Cataloging-in-Publication Data

Muszynski, Julie.
  The Red book of dogs / Julie Muszynski. -- 1st ed.
    p. cm.
  Includes index.
  ISBN-13: 978-0-06-123887-1 (hardcover)
  ISBN-10: 0-06-123887-2 (hardcover)
  1. Dogs. I. Title.

  SF426.M876 2007
  636.7'1--dc22

                                                    2006101737

Printed in China
First Printing, 2007

FOR MOM

My little dog—a heartbeat at my feet.

—Edith Warton

PREFACE

The Red Book of Dogs and its partner, *The Blue Book of Dogs* were inspired by the original titles written in 1939 by Robert Briggs Logan. Today, nearly three quarters of a century later, they return with their original breed descriptions, updated and enhanced with fun and interesting facts and additional images.

At dog shows, all breeds are divided into seven groups—sporting dogs, hounds, working dogs, herding dogs, terriers, toys, and non-sporting dogs. *The Red Book of Dogs* describes those breeds in the hound, terrier, and toy groups, while the partner to this book, *The Blue Book of Dogs,* includes sporting dogs, working dogs, herding dogs, and non-sporting dogs, all arranged alphabetically within their groups for quick reference.

The sport of breeding dogs throughout the centuries has resulted in the dog becoming an animal more diversified in appearance and value to man than any other living being. Dogs range in size from the one-pound Chihuahua to the two hundred-pound St. Bernard; from the stubby-legged Dachshund to the huge Irish Wolfhound standing as high as six feet on his hind legs. They may be almost any color, according to their breed.

The story of the dog goes back to the beginning of human history when dog aided man in his daily hunt for food. Through the ages, the dog has remained by the side of humans, helping to fight their battles, to guard their homes, and to serve in numerous other ways.

Today, the dog's service to humankind has narrowed to that for which he is better fitted than any other animal. He gives us, in this busy life, the balance we need through his day-in day-out companionship. No matter how great our worries, a dog's friendship and consistent loyalty never subsides; it soothes our ruffled feelings, eliminates our loneliness, restores our good spirits, and by actual example in trust, patience, and gratitude, gives us the courage to have continued confidence in humankind.

HOUNDS · TERRIERS · TOYS

AFGHAN HOUND
Hound

About 4000 B.C., Afghan Hounds played an important role in the lives of the Egyptians, coursing rabbits and helping in leopard hunts. There have even been assertions made that Noah carried a pair of Afghan Hounds aboard the Ark.

The Afghan Hound is one of the Greyhound family, which also includes the Saluki. His head is typically Greyhound, and though not as swift as his cousin, he can hold his own in racing with most other breeds.

This dog chooses his own friends. He is of a somewhat sensitive nature, but one finds him very attached to his own surroundings and more than curious if it becomes necessary to protect his home.

In appearance, the Afghan shows speed and power with a graceful outline. Weight is about sixty pounds, and height runs from twenty-five to twenty-seven inches when measured from the foreshoulder.

The breed did not surface in North America and Europe until the turn of the twentieth century, as the people of Afghanistan were reluctant to sell their national dog to foreigners.

Imported from Ghazni, Afghanistan, in 1931, Zeppo Marx's Afghan Hounds—Omar and Asra— are believed to be the first of this breed to have been brought to the United States.

An Afghan Hound named Suppy was the first dog ever to be cloned—by Korean scientist Hwang Woo-Suk, on August 3, 2005.

Pablo Picasso owned two Afghan Hounds, Kasbec and Kabul.

The Afghan's fur is long and full around his legs, resembling a pair of pants, which is why this breed is often referred to as the Hound in Pajamas.

AMERICAN FOXHOUND
Hound

The English Foxhound and the French Hound were crossed to originate a breed that lives for the sole purpose of chasing the fox over hill and dale in a pack with other hounds. The American Foxhound is most common throughout the southern part of the United States. The master can tell whether his dog has discovered the scent of the hunted fox or has lost it merely by listening to the deep-throated bay of his dog.

The American Foxhound is not a dog that wanders about aimlessly, but he tends to his own business and sleeps a great deal of the time. However, during the hunt he will keep going for some twelve hours at a stretch.

This breed can be any hound color, which usually includes patches of black or tan, or both, on a white body. The coat of the American Foxhound is close, hard, and of medium length.

In height, this breed is between twenty and twenty-five inches from the top of the shoulder to the ground.

The American Foxhound is Virginia's state animal.

The Walker Hound, Birdsong Hound, Henry Hound, and Hayden Trigg Hound are all recognized varieties of the American Foxhound.

George Washington is considered the father of the American Foxhound. It is believed that in the early 1800s, French soldier Marquis de Lafayette presented him with French Foxhounds. Washington bred the dogs with his own English Foxhounds, thus creating the present-day breed of the American Foxhound.

"It is said that this dog is capable of tiring out ten horses. Indeed, he can run around an area of ninety-three square miles without stopping from dawn to dusk, finally returning home perhaps in the middle of the night with energy to spare after lingering over the last lap."

—*The Great Book of Dogs*

BASSET HOUND
Hound

A genial disposition has caused the Basset Hound to be termed a lady's hound, though he is a real artist at flushing game. He is a gentleman of ease, the slowest of all hunting dogs, but deliberate.

The Basset Hound is a very likable companion and is being used more and more in North America to hunt raccoon, squirrel, and pheasant. The breed, like the Foxhound, is used to hunting in a pack and is best chasing after animals that require slow trailing.

The height of the Basset Hound is usually around fourteen inches; weight can be anywhere between twenty-five and forty pounds.

In appearance, this hound from France resembles a Beagle elongated into a near Dachshund. The coat is similar to that of the Foxhound in both texture and color.

The head resembles that of a Bloodhound. The skin of the Basset Hound is very loose and elastic.

In 1956, on *The Steve Allen Show*, Elvis Presley famously sang "Hound Dog" to a Basset Hound named Sherlock.

Biggles, the original Basset Hound mascot for Hush Puppies shoes, is grandfather to Mr. Jeffries, the dog that holds a place in the *Guinness Book of World Records* for the longest ears on a dog. At eleven and a half inches, these extensive ears often cause this pup to trip.

The Basset Hound derived its name from the French adjective *bas*, meaning "low."

A Basset Hound puppy was featured on the cover of *Time* magazine in 1928, accompanying an article about the 52nd annual Westminster Kennel Club Dog Show, which led to the breed's increased popularity in the United States.

Marilyn Monroe had a Basset Hound named Hugo.

BEAGLE
Hound

The Beagle is in reality a miniature Foxhound, the smallest, and the merriest, of the hound family. Few other breeds can equal the little Beagle's playful and happy temperament. It is even more pronounced during the chase, when he makes full use of his singing, bell-like voice. He is speedy for his size, making him a great hunter of hares.

Being all hound dog, the breed has hound colors. There are two varieties of this breed: The Thirteen Inch Beagle and the Fifteen Inch Beagle. Both should resemble a typical Foxhound in miniature. He is solid and big for those inches and possesses a never-give-up look of the hound out to find his quarry.

There is little known about the origin of the Beagle. Some say that the breed was created during Grecian times when rabbit and hare coursing was a favorite sport.

For several hundred years, this breed has been used in packs by English royalty, and it was mostly through their efforts that the Beagle has today become an ideal dog for both show and field.

President Lyndon B. Johnson owned five Beagles: Him, Her, Edgar, Beagle, and Little Beagle. He once caused a terrible ruckus by picking one of his pups up by its ears, upsetting not only the dog but his spectators as well.

Beagles make beagle music—a loud sound, bark, or howl—when in full pursuit.

It is said that during the Hundred Years' War, Edward III had a pack of up to 120 Beagles with him on the battlefield.

In the sixteenth century, a smaller version of Beagle was known as the Pocket Beagle because it could be carried in small baskets on hunters' saddlebags.

The most famous Beagle of all is Charles Schulz's Snoopy. Snoopy's siblings from Daisy Hill Puppy Farm are Spike, Belle, Marbles, Olaf, and Andy.

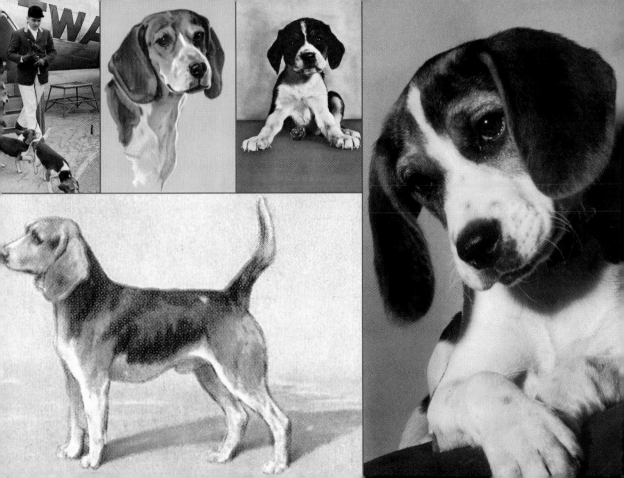

BLOODHOUND
Hound

Bloodhounds belie both their name and appearance. This ancient dog is not in the least barbarous, and although he is physically imposing, he is not mean or vicious.

The Bloodhound is a very easygoing dog except when the thrill of the chase comes over him. He has an acute sense of smell unparalleled by any other breed. For centuries, the nose of this breed has served man by trailing escaped prisoners after the tracks are days old. However, when the Bloodhound discovers that which he is after, he does not attack it but merely corners the prey and barks furiously until the posse arrives upon the scene.

The breed is so old that any qualified account of his origin is impossible. It is generally conceded that the first roamed throughout the Mediterranean area.

The wrinkled head, very long ears, and sad, sunken eyes make the Bloodhound distinctive in the canine family.

In eighteenth-century Belgium, Bloodhounds were called Saint Hubert Hounds, after the saint who made them popular.

This dog is sometimes called a Sleuthhound, as he is the only dog whose testimony is admissible as evidence in a court of law.

The famous English painting *Dignity and Impudence* by renowned artist Sir Edwin Landseer, features a Bloodhound in a doghouse with a little Cairn Terrier.

One of the most memorable Bloodhound characters is McGruff the Crime Dog, whose famous slogan was "Help take a bite out of crime."

There are two theories about the origin of the word Bloodhound. One refers to the uncanny ability to track the blood trail of a wounded animal; the other refers to his aristocratic bloodline.

BORZOI
Hound

The Borzoi is more popularly known as the Russian Wolfhound, which was the official name until 1936. *Borzoi* is the Russian name for the breed.

The Borzoi is the aristocrat of the dog world, elegant and graceful in appearance. Having strong endurance and great speed, he is a fine courser of wolves.

The coat of the Borzoi is long and silky, predominantly white with markings of any other color. Average height is about thirty inches; weight, from seventy-five to 105 pounds.

The Borzoi emphasizes the grace, beauty, and regal character befitting dogs of the breed that were such favorites during the reign of the Russian nobility.

Borzois own a quiet and rather undemonstrative personality but are easily trained; once a trick is learned, it is never forgotten.

The Borzoi, whose name means "fast" in Russian, made his appearance toward the end of the nineteenth century in Europe. Queen Victoria owned one, as did her daughter-in-law Alexandra, who later became queen. Alexandra was often photographed with her Borzoi, Ajax.

During the Art Deco period, French artist Louis Icart was renowned for his paintings of Borzoi.

For centuries, the only way to acquire a Borzoi was as a gift from a Russian czar.

It is thought that a Russian duke imported Salukis from Arabia in the 1600s and crossed them with Collies, thus creating the Borzoi.

A member of the Greyhound family, the Borzoi is not only very beautiful but also an excellent sight hound.

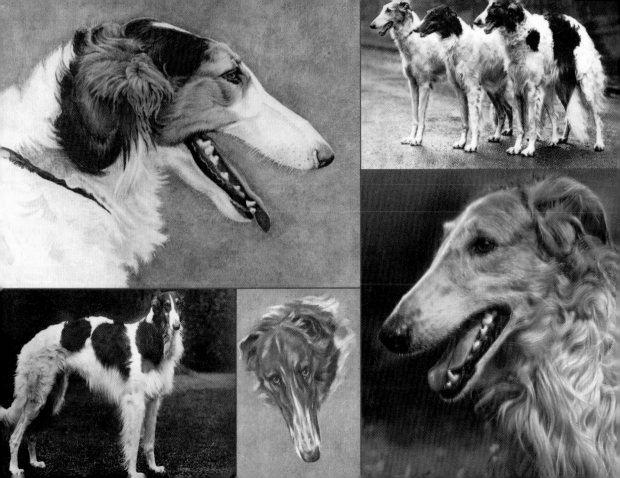

DACHSHUND
LONGHAIRED VARIETY
Hound

The Dachshund is affectionately known as the dog that is a dog high and two dogs long. His name explains his original use; *Dachs* is German for "badger," while *Hund* is German for "dog." This breed has the scenting instincts of the hound and the size of the terrier, making him an excellent hunter of ground animals.

There are three varieties of the Dachshund, which differ only in coat—the longhaired, the smooth, and the wirehaired. Of these, the smooth is the most popular. The longhaired variety owns a coat of silky texture, slightly waved and with rather pronounced feathering on his legs and tail.

The Dachshund came into popularity several hundred years ago and has retained that popularity through a strong and lovable personality.

To avoid any connection with its native Germany during the postwar years, the Dachshund was temporarily referred to as the Badger Dog in the United States.

Gergwies, Germany, is known as the Dachshund capital of the world; tourists can rent Dachshunds by the hour for private walks.

Mickey Mouse's dog, Pluto, was in love with a Dachshund named Dinah.

Napoleon Bonaparte had his portrait painted with Grenouille, one of his many Dachshunds.

The Dachshund is one of the top ten most popular dog breeds in the United States.

DACHSHUND
SMOOTH VARIETY
Hound

The variety of the Dachshund most frequently seen in North America is the Smooth. Colors are usually either solid red or black and tan. The coat is short and dense.

The short-legged dog that resembles the Bloodhound to some degree is a vigorous and almost tireless worker. He possesses a strong quality of courageousness, and, although he can stand up under a most severe attack, he will not force a quarrel with another dog or be disagreeably aggressive.

With the Bloodhound power of scent, the low-slung Dachshund is a fine watchdog. He detects the faintest sounds quickly and gives warning immediately. He makes a splendid house dog and amuses his family for many funny hours with his playful antics, amusing poses, and general good-hearted fun.

Newspaper magnate William Randolph Hearst famously installed a tiny ladder in the swimming pool at Hearst Castle for his Dachshund, Helena.

Napoleon Bonaparte owned many Dachshunds that he loved fiercely. A true narcissist, he named one of his little pets after himself. Like his owner, Napoleon the Dachshund tried to make up for his small stature with a bold, assertive personality. Sounds like he had a Napoleon complex.

In 1839, Prince Albert presented a Dachshund as a gift to his wife, Queen Victoria, whom she appropriately named Dash. There is a bronze statue at Windsor Castle of Boy, another of the queen's beloved Dachshunds.

After the filming of *Cleopatra*, Elizabeth Taylor presented her husband, Richard Burton, with an entire litter of Dachshunds.

DACHSHUND

WIREHAIRED VARIETY

Hound

The coat of the Wirehaired Dachshund differs, in addition to his bristly coat, in color, for any color is permissible. Certain authorities have concluded that this variety came into existence as a result of crossing the Smooth Dachshund with the Irish Terrier; however, this can only be presumed, as there are no records to authenticate it.

Both of these types are useful dogs in the field. They are excellent hunters of rabbit, woodchuck, fox, and all animals that live in the ground. They can easily enter a hole, kill the most ferocious animal, and bring it back to the surface. They are good trackers and can follow any game providing it does not require too speedy traveling.

The weight of the Dachshund can vary from the miniature Dachshund, which is bred in all three coats and weighs up to nine pounds, to the standard Dachshund, which can weigh between sixteen and thirty-two pounds.

The Dachshund appears to have developed in Germany more than three hundred years ago, though his ancestry can be traced back to ancient Egyptian times through hieroglyphics.

In Germany, this breed is referred to by name as *Tackel* or *Dackel*, meaning "sausage dog."

In the fourteenth, fifteenth, and sixteenth centuries, popes were believed to have kept Dachshunds, which were referred to as altar dogs. Their varieties remain uncertain.

In Munich, West Germany, in 1972, Waldi the Dachshund was officially named the Olympic mascot.

Leonardo da Vinci owned a Dachshund, which, coincidentally, was named Mona.

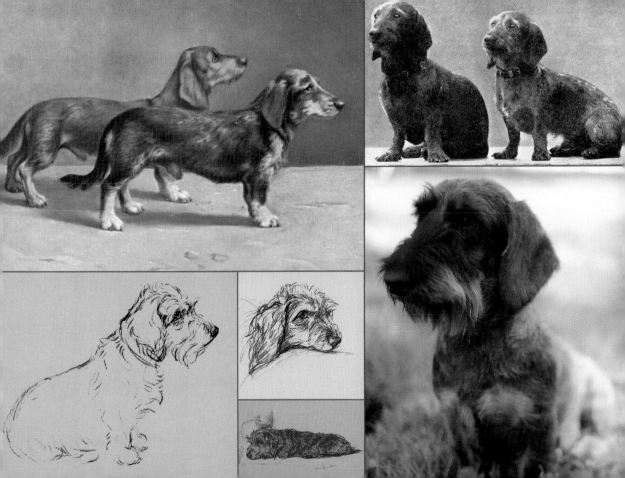

ENGLISH FOXHOUND
Hound

The English Foxhound differs from his younger cousin, the American Foxhound, principally in size. Though this dog is several inches higher than the American, he is not rangy.

This breed always runs in packs when fox hunting, long a popular sport in England. A pack of Foxhounds presents a beautiful sight as they run over hill and dale after the escaping fox, followed by the red-coated huntsmen on horseback.

English Foxhounds have been bred very exactly in England for more than150 years, being always under careful supervision.

Few breeds can parallel a good English Foxhound in combined strength, grace, and beauty while running. The coat is short, dense, and rather glossy, of normal hound colors, including black or tan with white and patches of a third color.

During Henry VIII's reign in the late 1500s, the deer population had become severely depleted and a new prey, the fox, was chosen. It was at this point that the English Foxhound was developed by carefully mixing the Greyhound, the English Bulldog, and the Fox Terrier.

There has been much debate in the United Kingdom over parliament's institution of the Hunting Act in 2004, which banned hunting with dogs.

English Foxhound studbooks—which chronicle the lineage of this breed—have been kept as early as the 1800s.

In 1935, *Hutchinson's Encyclopaedia* described the English Foxhound varieties as follows: "The White—was used mostly for stag-hunting. The Fallow—was used for hunting all sorts of quarry, principally the stag. The Dunn—the commonest breed, and would hunt any game. The Black or St. Hubert—forbearer of the Bloodhound and Southern Hound."

GREYHOUND
Hound

The title "swiftest of all dogs" belongs to the Greyhound. No other breed can match him in speed. The Greyhound is built for speed and widely used as a racing dog, though originally, in western Asia, he was a courser of gazelles, antelopes, and other, similar animals.

These dogs weigh from sixty to seventy pounds and stand twenty-seven to thirty inches in height.

In spite of his size, the Greyhound makes a good dog for the home, being clean in his habits and short-haired. He is not a vicious dog, nor is he cowardly. Unlike many other breeds, the Greyhound can withstand both heat and cold. He is found all over the world.

Greyhounds are very old, originating about 4000 B.C. in Egypt, where they were the favorite of the royalty.

The Greyhound is closely related to other coursers such as the Afghan Hound, Borzoi, Irish Wolfhound, Saluki, Scottish Deerhound, and the Whippet.

The second-fastest land animal after the cheetah, Greyhounds can reach the speed of 45 miles per hour within one and a half seconds.

This breed is mentioned in eleven of Shakespeare's plays and is the only breed of dog mentioned in the Bible.

In Homer's *Odyssey*, Odysseus has a Greyhound named Argus.

General George A. Custer was extremely fond of the Greyhound, and said to have traveled with a pack of forty.

Al Capone, Bo Derek, Merv Griffin, Jerry Lewis, Dean Martin, Babe Ruth, Frank Sinatra, and Ed Sullivan have all owned Greyhounds. John Barrymore is said to have owned eleven. Frederick the Great had fifteen.

HARRIER
Hound

The Harrier is a pack hunter but has also been used to hunt singly. The breed closely resembles Foxhounds, although having a more stocky body and shorter legs. Bloodhound ancestry shows in his long ears, kind facial expression, and keen scent, but his actual origin is mystifying. This dog is a superb hunter of hares, having been used for this sport for at least two-thousand years.

The coat of the Harrier is flat and smooth, colored black and tan with white, or any hound colors. He weighs about forty-five pounds and is about twenty inches high.

In addition to his similarity in appearance to the Foxhound, the Harrier also works much like that breed. He is slower, but is exceptionally good for the drag hunt, which requires a slower pace. The popularity of the Harrier in England is due to the fact that he can be followed on foot instead of horseback while hunting in packs, making it possible for the middle class to enjoy this famous sport.

The breed's name, Harrier, refers to its ability to hunt hare.

Detailed records dating from 1260 reveal the history of the earliest Harrier packs in England.

"No other dog can equal his ability in hunting down hare. He combines a faultless sense of smell with the speed of an athlete and an impressive vitality. He can run sixteen miles at full speed without stopping."
—*The Great Book of Dogs*

Hare hunting fell out of style in the late 1960s, giving way to the more popular sport of fox hunting and contributing to the dwindling numbers of Harriers today.

Harriers are one of the rarest dog breeds; there are only four to five litters born in the United States each year.

IRISH WOLFHOUND
Hound

Irish Wolfhounds are oftentimes spoken of as the Great Dog of Ireland. They are the mascots for the Irish Guard.

Though ancient breed, the Irish Wolfhound as he is seen today did not exist until 1860, when the old, bulky type was bred with the Scottish Deerhound, Great Dane, Russian Wolfhound (Borzoi), and others.

The Irish Wolfhound is the longest of all dogs. When standing on his hind legs, he usually reaches a height of six feet or more. Dogs must not be under thirty-two inches high or weigh less than 120 pounds, though females may be slightly smaller.

The Irish Wolfhound's immense length gives him a regal appearance. He is fearful of nothing and yet is one of the gentlest of all dogs.

Irish Wolfhounds are called by many names, such as Big Dogs of Ireland, Great Hounds of Ireland, Wolfdogs of Ireland, and Irish Dogs.

"Today's Wolfhound has shown himself to be an excellent guard-dog. He does not bite, but with his imposing size and bark he holds his victims at bay. If instructed to attack, he can kill a man."
—*The Great Book of Dogs*

Two U.S. presidents owned Wolfhounds: Herbert Hoover had one named Patrick, and John F. Kennedy had one named Wolf.

Irish Wolfhounds are the tallest of all dog breeds; females reach thirty to thirty-two inches, while males are generally thirty-two to thirty-four inches.

At the Gettysburg National Military Park in Pennsylvania, there is a monument of an Irish Wolfhound lying beneath a Celtic cross, in memory of the members of the Irish Brigade who died in the Battle of Gettysburg in 1863.

NORWEGIAN ELKHOUND
Hound

This dog is distinctive in that he has been bred true to type since the Viking age, the eighth to the eleventh centuries, when he was used for the hunt of elk, boar, and bear in the deep forests of Sweden and Norway. He is an Arctic type, has often pulled sledges, and can withstand the coldest weather.

The Norwegian Elkhound is sometimes confused with the Keeshond, which he so closely resembles in general appearance. The color of his coarse, abundant coat is gray in various shades. He carries his tail tightly curled over his back in a manner typical of the Arctic breeds.

The weight of this dog is about fifty pounds. He stands about twenty inches high. The Norwegian Elkhound is a friendly dog, possessing great intelligence and stamina. Though a real outdoors dog, he is clean in his habits and makes a companionable house dog of remarkably gentle disposition and with little or no show of nervousness. He is a fine friend.

Norwegian Elkhounds are one of the oldest breeds of dogs. Archaeological digs in Scandinavia suggest these dogs lived and were domesticated as far back as the Stone Age.

This breed's name originates from the Norwegian word *Elghund* meaning "moosedog."

An Elkhound can detect elk by smell at a distance of two to three miles.

When hunting, the Elkhound is known for his ability to avoid the elk's massive horns with fast and vigorous movements, alerting the hunter to impending danger by uniquely changing the tone of his bark.

President Herbert Hoover had a Norwegian Elkhound named Weejie.

OTTERHOUND
Hound

As the name suggests, this breed is used to hunt otter, a sport in which he excels due to his ability to fight in water. The Otterhound's webbed feet make him a very strong swimmer. He is more than willing to battle any and all water quarry.

Originally from France and England, the actual breeds, other than the Southern Hound, used to develop this great water dog are shrouded in mystery. He appears to be a blend of the Foxhound and the Bloodhound when coat is not considered. His hair is longish, hard, rather crisp, and water-resistant, and is colored blue and white through various shades of black and tan. He is a good-sized breed, standing twenty-four to twenty-seven inches and weighing as much as 115 pounds.

He possesses an unfailing devotion and a sagacity of character all his own. As a killer of the fighting otter and as a powerful underwater swimmer, the Otterhound can hold his own against all other breeds of hunting dogs.

Related to the Bloodhound, the Otterhound is a rough-haired version of its cousin. The breed is often described as the Bloodhound in Sheep's Clothing.

There are approximately 350 Otterhounds in existence in North America and fewer than one thousand worldwide.

Many kings have owned Otterhounds, but it was Queen Elizabeth I who was referred to as Lady Master of the Otterhounds.

For more than seven hundred years, the Otterhound has been used to control the otter population, thus protecting the lives of many fish.

SALUKI
Hound

Also named the Persian Gazelle Hound, the Saluki is the royal dog of Egypt—the Greyhound of the desert. Arabs have used the Saluki for coursing gazelles and hares for thousands of years.

Were it not for the Saluki's feathered ears, tail, and legs, he could easily be mistaken for a Greyhound, for he has the grace, symmetry, and speed of that racing dog. Colors of his silky coat vary from white through cream, to grizzle and black, including combinations. His height is twenty-three to twenty-eight inches.

The Saluki is a hardy dog, well muscled, and capable of running quickly over sand for long distances. Due probably to his association with Egyptian royalty through the centuries, the Saluki is a picture of regality, and his personality is aristocratic. He is both gentle and dignified—an affectionate dog without being overly demonstrative. He is a fine watchdog.

This breed is named after the vanished city of Saluki in the Middle East.

In the Muslim world, the Saluki is a sacred gift of Allah, only given as a token of friendship and never to be sold.

The Saluki is Southern Illinois University's mascot for all of its sports teams.

Salukis are known for their cleanliness; they are the only breed of dog the Bedouin do not consider unclean.

"Salukis were widespread and appeared in Egypt, where they were held in such great esteem that their bodies were often mummified like the bodies of the pharaohs themselves."

—American Kennel Club

SCOTTISH DEERHOUND
Hound

The Scottish Deerhound closely resembles the Irish Wolfhound, having probably been created from this large breed and the old hounds of the Picts or the Greyhound, whose general outlines are quite similar. He is a courageous and dependable courser of deer, a graceful dog in movement, and a real aristocrat of the canine family.

The breed is impressive in size, weighing from seventy-five to 110 pounds and standing twenty-eight inches or more in height. His coat is outstanding in that it is more than three inches long and wiry. It is self-colored, being any color but white. A dark blue-gray is preferred.

The Scottish Deerhound is a splendid breed for the country estate. His distinctive size is of value in guarding the grounds, a duty in which he is exceedingly capable. He has an excellent disposition and loves to be near people.

This breed made a striking appearance in the film *Out of Africa* as the companion of the Baroness Karen von Blixen, played by Meryl Streep.

"Beneath the sculptured form which late you wore, sleep soundly, Maida, at your master's door."
—Sir Walter Scott's inscription on the monument of his Deerhound, Maida

Historically, no one beneath an earl was allowed to possess ownership and breeding privileges of a Deerhound, ultimately threatening the extinction of this breed.

Strong and determined, one of these dogs can bring down a deer weighing as much as 250 pounds.

WHIPPET
Hound

As a racer, the Whippet is surpassed only by the swiftest of dogs, the Greyhound. It has been said that he was either bred down from the Greyhound or bred up from the Italian Greyhound; however, this is generally conceded to be untrue. The Whippet stands from eighteen to twenty-two inches high and usually weighs from twelve to twenty-eight pounds.

Though from his streamlined body one would believe this racer to be fragile, he is decidedly hardy and possesses great stamina. He is a graceful dog and plucky in chasing rabbits.

This English dog has a very close coat that may be any color and is as clean-cut in appearance as that of any other breed. He is exceptionally faithful to his owner and adds to this a superb intelligence, due possibly to the presence of Manchester Terrier blood. The Whippet is a clean dog for the house and easily adapts himself to numerous modes of living. He has many desirable canine characteristics.

The Whippet is capable of racing at speeds ranging from thirty-five to forty miles per hour and is rumored to run a 200-yard track in twelve seconds.

A Whippet named Ashley Whippet (after the character Ashley Wilkes in *Gone with the Wind*) is considered to be one of the greatest Frisbee dogs of all time. In the 1970s, he won three world championships, performed at the White House and Super Bowl XII, and starred in an Academy Award–nominated documentary *Floating Free*.

The name Whippet is believed to have originated from the Middle Low German and Middle Dutch word *wippen*, meaning "to move quickly."

The Whippet was known as the poor man's Greyhound and became a favorite of British miners who bet their weekly pay on these speedy dogs.

Whippets were also nicknamed Rag Dogs, as their owners were known to wave rags at them during a race, encouraging them to run faster.

AIREDALE TERRIER
Terrier

Friends of the Airedale Terrier have named him the King of the Terriers. The breed is not the heaviest of the terrier clan but, in height, is the largest. It is one of the numerous breeds coming from the British Isles, having originated in the Aire Valley during the nineteenth century.

The Airedale is a beautiful dog, with his head and tail held erect; with his hard, wiry coat; with his body a black or dark grizzly color; and his forequarters and legs a rich tan.

In temperament, the Airedale is terrierlike. He is forward in his feelings and daring in the fight. He is absolutely unafraid.

No other breed owns a more lovable, undeceitful nature. In addition to this, the Airedale Terrier can be trained for numerous uses. In police work, in hunting, and even as a war dog, the Airedale has long proved himself to be a very useful servant of humankind.

After World War I, the Airedale became popular due to its brave service and conduct in the war. The breed was known to persevere and carry out orders even while wounded.

Three consecutive U.S. presidents owned Airedale Terriers: Woodrow Wilson had Davie; Warren Harding had Laddie Boy; and Calvin Coolidge had Paul Pry (originally Laddie Buck), Laddie Boy's half brother. Laddie Boy was said to have his own carved chair in the White House and was often quoted by the press in mock interviews. The Smithsonian Institution houses a statue of this beloved pooch made from nineteen thousand melted newsboys' pennies.

It is believed that two Airedale Terriers belonging to John Jacob Astor perished when the *Titanic* sank.

Other famous Airedale owners include John Steinbeck and John Wayne, who owned Little Duke.

BEDLINGTON TERRIER

Terrier

A dog distinctive in appearance is the Bedlington Terrier. He is the lamb of the canine family but is far from this when his personality is considered.

This terrier breed, like the Dandie Dinmont Terrier, combines the Otterhound and the Border Terrier, and probably Whippet blood. The coat is lamblike, being very closely knit and woolly. Colors are varied with a bluish gray most common. Other colors are blue and tan, liver and tan, sandy and tan, or solid liver.

The Bedlington Terrier is a great hunter of vermin, and no other breed surpasses it in pure grit. It must not be supposed from the above inferences that the Bedlington is a tough dog, for he is docile and makes a fine pet, being every bit as affectionate and loyal to home as other breeds are. He is not a mischief-maker, but neither does he ask for sympathy and help.

The height of this breed is about fifteen inches; the weight is between seventeen and twenty-three pounds.

The first known Bedlington Terrier was said to have been owned by Joseph Ainsley of Bedlington, England, hence the breed's name.

This terrier has been nicknamed the Miner's Racehorse because miners gathered after work to stage rat-catching competitions, which evolved into racing competitions.

Due to his feisty personality and sweet face, this little dog is often acknowledged as having a lion's heart and a lamb's face.

It is rumored that in the eighteenth century, these terriers were unique to the gypsies in the Rothbury Forest area of England, thus giving the breed the nickname Gypsy Dog.

Dorothy Parker owned a Bedlington Terrier named Wolf.

BORDER TERRIER

Terrier

Border Terriers were designed for use rather than for beauty. They are definitely a sporting type of terrier from northern England, having been used there for many years to hunt vermin, foxes, and other animals. The breed probably originated from the cross-breeding of the Bedlington Terrier and the Dandie Dinmont Terrier. He weighs between eleven and fifteen pounds.

As with other sporting terriers, this hearty dog is a brave one, with jaws capable of biting severely. The color of the Border Terrier is always reddish. He has two coats—the outercoat dense and harsh, the undercoat thick—so he can withstand much punishment.

Most of the terrier clan is strong in courage, and the Border Terrier has his share. He is game, active, and intelligent in performing his duties as a hunter of ground animals. He is a tireless worker with a stick-to-it-iveness that keeps him after the hunted fox until it is captured, regardless of any perils he might meet with during the chase.

This breed originated between the borders of England and Scotland, hence the name Border Terrier.

Dating back to the eighteenth century, the Border Terrier is recognized as one of the oldest of all terrier breeds.

Stars of the film *There's Something About Mary*, Ben Stiller and a Border Terrier named Puffy, won the 1999 MTV Movie Award for Best Fight Sequence in a film.

A very strong chewer, the Border Terrier can remove the noise-making mechanism from a squeaky toy within thirty seconds.

BULL TERRIER
COLORED VARIETY
Terrier

There are two varieties of the Bull Terrier, the difference being only in color of the coat. The breed originated in England probably from the Bulldog and the now extinct English Terrier. He is classed as a terrier but in conformation resembles more closely the Bulldog types.

Bull Terriers are the professional pugilists of dogdom, having been used for badger baiting and pit fighting almost exclusively before this cruel sport was outlawed. The Bull Terrier is a sturdy fighter capable of keeping a deathlike grip on his adversary until the other is slain. The breed is also a great killer of vermin.

The facial expression of the Bull Terrier makes one believe that he is always laughing, and he is good-natured in spite of his reputation for fighting. Both grace and strength show in his body movement.

President Theodore Roosevelt's Bull Terrier, Pete, was famously banished from the White House after he attacked a French ambassador.

Both varieties of Bull Terriers are identical except for color, and both can be born within the same litter.

The colored Bull Terrier is believed to be a descendant of both the Staffordshire Bull Terrier and the pure White Bull Terrier.

According to *Hutchinson's Encyclopaedia*, "Brindle dogs are acceptable; red dogs are understandable; but parti-colored dogs of black-and-tan-and-white and other variations of the rainbow are as difficult to harness to the imagination as is the rainbow to the earth."

A colored Bull Terrier named Rufus won Best in Show at the 2006 Westminster Dog Show.

BULL TERRIER
WHITE VARIETY
Terrier

The chalky color of the white variety of the Bull Terrier has presented him with the nickname, the White Cavalier. This dog and the colored variety differ only in color.

The Bull Terrier possesses an ideal disposition. He loves to play and makes a fine companion for a child. However, he owns a reputation for being a terrific fighting dog. The Bull Terrier will not be frightened; he knows no fear. No matter what his enemy might be: trespasser, another dog, or raging bull, he will not retreat but will stand his position.

As for size, this standard Bull Terrier can weigh anywhere from forty-five to eighty pounds and measure twenty to twenty-four inches in height. The miniature Bull Terrier weighs between twenty-four and thirty-three pounds and can measure between ten and fifteen inches in height.

The head of the Bull Terrier is long, flat, and wide between the ears, with powerful jaws capable of giving severe punishment.

In the beginning of the nineteenth century, it was fashionable for Bull Terriers to compete in the sport of dogfighting, and sportsmen bred them with this competitive spirit in mind. This brutal sport was eventually banned in England.

"It is truly termed the gladiator of the canine race, and some consider it to be one of the most handsome dogs of all time."
—*Dogs*

At the General Patton Memorial Museum in California, there is a twelve-foot-high bronze statue of Patton and his beloved Bull Terrier, Willie.

Other famous Bull Terriers include Spuds McKenzie, the Bud Light Beer mascot and America's Favorite Party Animal, and Bullseye, the dog in Target Corporation's logo.

The Bull Terrier is the only breed of dog with triangular-shaped eyes.

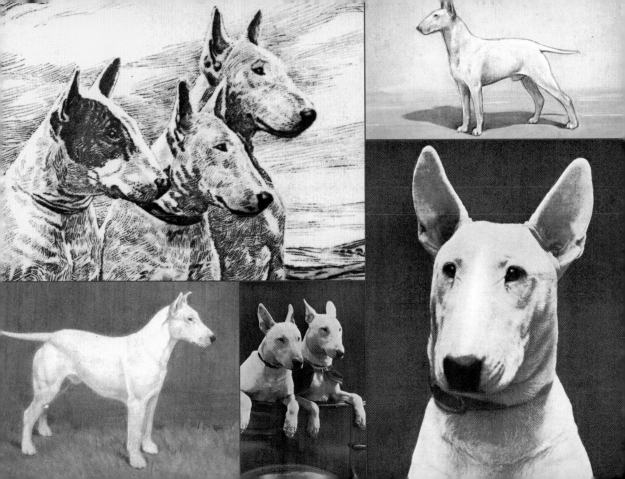

CAIRN TERRIER

Terrier

An extremely expressive face is the outstanding feature of this Britain from the Isle of Skye. The Cairn Terrier is a merry little chap and very hardy. He is the smallest of the terriers, having been bred for the select purpose of rushing game out of rocky cliffs.

This breed, although he is of the terrier clan, is not boisterous and attends fairly well to his own business, thus making him a splendid house dog.

The Cairn should be a certain weight for show purposes—fourteen pounds for the male and thirteen pounds for the female. Height should be between nine and ten inches. The breed has a double coat. A fury, close undercoat is covered by hard, weather-resistant hair of any color but white. The ears, muzzle, and tip of the tail have a darker tinge.

The Cairn Terrier is a devoted companion to his master but has little to do with strangers. He is quiet and has a very amiable disposition. He makes a splendid playmate for a child.

This terrier is named after the cairn, symbolic stone markers that covered graves in Scotland. The Cairn Terrier became useful for ridding the graves of unwanted vermin seeking shelter there.

The most famous Cairn Terrier is Toto, Dorothy's beloved companion in the 1939 film *The Wizard of Oz*. Terry, the female dog that played Toto, was the only feature character actor in the film who was paid less than its young star, Judy Garland.

Judy Garland's daughter, Liza Minnelli, owned a Cairn Terrier named Lily.

A very independent breed, Cairn Terriers do not make good lapdogs. Unlike Toto, real-life Cairn Terriers would object to being carried around in a basket.

DANDIE DINMONT TERRIER
Terrier

The Dandie Dinmont Terrier is different from all other breeds in appearance. He is a dog of curves, with a long body and a massive head that seems too large for his body. The coat of the Dandie Dinmont Terrier is long, crisp, and easy-flowing, colored either gray or mustard yellow.

This terrier breed is quiet and reserved. He has the dignity of the terrier clan that Sir Walter Scott popularized and, in fact, named in his novel *Guy Mannering*. The Dandie Dinmont Terrier probably came from a crossing of the Bedlington Terrier and the Border Terrier in England and Scotland some three hundred years ago. He is a dog that minds his own business but will stick up for his rights whenever the need arises.

He is a capable fighter and can hold his own with any dog in his weight class of about eighteen to twenty-four pounds. He stands from eight to eleven inches in height, and is rather low-slung.

Named after a farmer who owned six terriers in Sir Walter Scott's novel *Guy Mannering*, the Dandie Dinmont Terrier is the only breed that takes his name from literature.

The breed was originally known as Dandie Dinmont's Terriers, but the apostrophe and the "s" have since been dropped.

A notable characteristic of the Dandie Dinmont Terrier is his unique silvery white crown of hair that resembles a toupee.

Famous portraits of these dogs include Sir Edwin Landseer's *Sir Walter Scott* and Thomas Gainsborough's *Henry, Third Duke of Buccleuch*.

Gypsies and farmers originally raised these dogs to hunt and kill vermin.

FOX TERRIER
SMOOTH-HAIRED VARIETY
Terrier

The two types of Fox Terrier, smooth-haired and wirehaired, are among the liveliest of all the breeds of dogdom. This dog is another of England's and Ireland's numerous breeds. It has been used as a part of the hunt since the breed came into being in about 1840. The Fox Terrier goes after the fox when it has been driven into a hole or burrow by the hounds, kills it, and brings it to the hunting party.

Breeds used for the development of the Fox Terrier include the Manchester Terrier, English Terrier, Bull Terrier, Whippet, and some hound such as the Beagle or the Harrier.

The Fox Terrier is a good house dog with an affectionate and lovable disposition. He makes friends with all and attracts much attention as he struts down the street, pretending to be unafraid of man or beast. He learns tricks easily, makes a good watchdog, giving warning upon hearing the slightest sound, and is a splendid killer of vermin.

The French word *terrier* means "to burrow" and is a derivative of the Latin *terra* and the French *terre*, both meaning "earth."

Nipper, the famous trademark of His Master's Voice phonograph records, was a Smooth Fox Terrier.

President Herbert Hoover had two Fox Terriers: Big Ben and Sonnie.

Fox Terriers have often been the subject matter of artists—Maude Earl, Arthur Wardle, John Emms, and Cecil Aldin, to name a few.

A Smooth Fox Terrier named Ch. Warren Remedy was the only dog to have won Best in Show at the Westminster Dog Show three times consecutively, in 1907, 1908, and 1909.

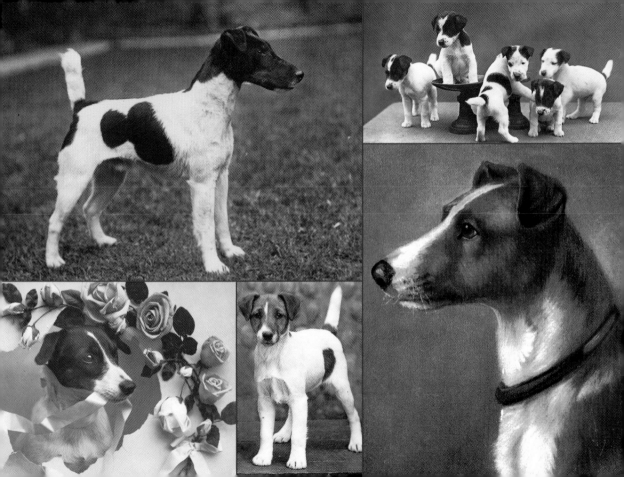

FOX TERRIER

WIREHAIRED VARIETY

Terrier

Wirehaired and Smooth-Haired Fox Terriers look quite different, due to the wide difference in their coats. The wirehaired variety is the younger of the two. It is believed that the wirehaired may have come from an old rough-coated black and tan terrier of Wales. Oddly, there may be smooth offspring of a mother and father, even if both are wirehaired. The opposite is also true.

In personality, the wirehaired is just as merry and tenacious as the smooth and is every bit as lovable.

White is the predominating color of the Fox Terrier, with markings of black or brown, or both present, though color is of little importance. Both varieties of the Fox Terrier weigh about eighteen pounds and should not stand more than fifteen inches high.

This breed is afraid of nothing and is ever looking for adventure. He is the spirit of youth, ready for anything, and makes a real pal for an active child.

When King Edward VII died, his Wire Fox Terrier, Caesar, led the funeral procession, walking in front of princes and kings.

This breed became a popular household pet in the 1930s, when Asta, a Wire Fox Terrier, starred as the family dog in the *Thin Man* films. Asta went on to appear in screwball comedies, including *The Awful Truth* and *Bringing Up Baby*, acting alongside other great actors, such as Cary Grant and Katharine Hepburn.

Snowy—a Wire Fox Terrier—was the pet of European comic character Tin Tin and accompanied him on his worldwide adventures.

The Wire Fox Terrier has received more Best in Show titles at major dog shows than any other breed.

IRISH TERRIER

Terrier

The Irish Terrier is one of three breeds so closely related that at a glance one can hardly tell them apart. The other two are the Airedale and the Welsh Terrier.

The Irish Terrier's bravery has earned him the nickname the Daredevil. He loves to fight and is ever merry and lively. Tender toward those he loves, he will give his very life to protect his home and family.

The Irish Terrier's coat is rough and wiry, and whole—colored wheaten, red, or golden red, the last being preferred. Weight averages twenty-five to twenty-seven pounds; height is about eighteen inches.

This great little dog loves the water and can easily be taught to retrieve. Really, there is nothing the Irish Terrier does not love to do. He fears absolutely nothing, regardless of size. For a watchdog plus companion, the Irish Terrier is a good breed.

This breed originated in County Cork, Ireland.

The Irish Terrier is the only member of the terrier family noted for his red coat.

The Irish Terrier was used as a messenger and a sentinel during World War I.

Years ago, the University of Notre Dame's football team mascot was an Irish Terrier. Until 1963, these dogs could be seen on the sidelines of the game, along with the team.

KERRY BLUE TERRIER

Terrier

The national dog of Ireland is the Kerry Blue Terrier, famed for his stalwart heart and gentle nature. The Kerry is a terrier at fighting and a master at giving affection. He is also famed for his color, which is the rarest of all dog colors—blue. Though seeming to be wiry, the coat of the Kerry is soft, wavy, and quite silky.

It is believed that the Kerry Blue Terrier came into existence as a result of repeated crosses with the Bedlington Terrier, Dandy Dinmont Terrier, Irish Terrier, and possibly some unknown dog of another terrier type.

The Kerry Blue Terrier is an all-around dog. He is a good vermin hunter, guard dog, and herder. In addition to this, he has proved himself to be a good retriever for both land and water. This is rare for a terrier. As a companion dog for the home in the country or the city apartment, it is hard to find a better dog than the Kerry.

The Kerry Blue Terrier is named after the mountainous region in Ireland, County Kerry.

Ch. Torums Scarf Michael—a Kerry Blue Terrier nicknamed Mick—won Best in Show at the 2003 Westminster Dog Show.

Margaret Wise Brown, author of the children's classic *Goodnight Moon*, had a Kerry Blue Terrier named Crispan. He was the inspiration for her book *Mr. Dog: The Dog Who Belonged to Himself.*

Kerry Blue Terriers are born black at birth, but their color fades to a blue gray by the time they are eighteen months old.

Ethel and John Barrymore, Truman Capote, Bill Cosby, Alfred Hitchcock, and Mickey Rooney all owned Kerry Blue Terriers.

LAKELAND TERRIER
Terrier

This quiet-dispositioned terrier from England was formerly called the Patterdale Terrier and is also known as the Ullswater Terrier. He strongly resembles the Welsh Terrier, though he is slightly smaller. Weight should not exceed seventeen pounds; height, fourteen inches.

The Lakeland Terrier has frequently been used to work with the hound packs for the purpose of entering the burrow to kill the fox after it has been cornered by the pack. He is a game and courageous sporting terrier with extremely rapid movement.

The coat of the Lakeland is hard, dense, and wiry. It is colored blue, blue and tan, black and tan, red, mustard, grizzle and black, or wheaten. This breed and the Kerry Blue Terrier are the only terriers in which blue is allowed.

The Lakeland Terrier, due to his handy size and type of coat, is clean about the house and makes a good all-around pet for both child and adult.

The Lakeland Terrier originated in Cumberland County, England, due to the need to protect sheep from fox.

This breed is also known as the Cumberland, the Fell, and the West Moreland.

Bill Cosby is the famous owner of the Lakeland Terrier, Champion Revelry's Awesome Blossom, the top-winning Lakeland Terrier in the history of the breed.

In 1967, a Lakeland Terrier named Champion Stingray of Derryabah became the only dog ever to have won both the prestigious Westminster and Crufts dog shows.

LHASA APSO
Terrier

The Lhasa Apso closely resembles an Old English Sheepdog in miniature. The coat is quite long and of shaggy appearance. Like the Old English Sheepdog, his hair falls over the eyes. Color of the Lhasa varies from golden to black and parti-colors; however, the most preferred are lionlike colors, as he is the true Tibetan lion-dog. The Lhasa Apso comes from Tibet and a number of other sections of that part of the world.

This breed is almost toy in size, standing about ten inches at the shoulder. Lhasas make fine watchdogs for inside the home. They are exceedingly clean. They are very alert and wary of any strangers.

The Lhasa Apso truly loves his family and ever desires to please and be obedient. He does not like pampering, such as one might expect from a dog his size. He likes nothing better than a good, hard run out in the open.

The Lhasa was originally known as the *Abso Send Kye*, meaning the "bark lion sentinel dog," and was also called the Lhassa Terrier.

Lhasa Apsos were highly treasured in Tibet, bred to guard monasteries and temples from evil. The dogs are considered sacred, and it was believed that upon the death of a Lhasa Apso's master, his soul would enter the dog's body.

Liberace had seventeen dogs, one of which was a Lhasa Apso named Chop Suey.

Lhasa Apsos were considered to be good luck in Tibet.

MANCHESTER TERRIER
Terrier

This English-developed terrier is often referred to as the Black-and-Tan Terrier or Rat Terrier. The Manchester Terrier is in reality a small Doberman Pinscher, having had much to do with perfecting the Doberman. The Manchester's coat is shiny and short, colored the same as that of his larger cousin. It is believed that the Manchester Terrier is the result of crosses with several terrier breeds and the Whippet, which gives him his raciness and alertness.

The Manchester Terrier is a good, general all-purpose dog for the home as well as for hunting—having an excellent disposition and being a most satisfactory size. He ranges anywhere from twelve to twenty-two pounds in weight.

Whippet blood gives him speed and this, added to his gameness and intelligence, makes the Manchester a good hunter of rabbits, besides being a splendid vermin killer. Few breeds can parallel this terrier in grace and daintiness of gait.

Agatha Christie owned two Manchester Terriers—her first was Treacle and her second, Bingo, which inspired Hannibal, the canine character in her book *Postern of Fate*.

A Manchester Terrier named Billy was reported to have killed one hundred rats in only six minutes.

"In the 1850s, Her Majesty the Queen Victoria appointed Jack Black an accomplished Black and Tan breeder, as the Royal Ratcatcher."
—The British Manchester Terrier Club

While president, Theodore Roosevelt owned a Manchester Terrier, which he named Black Jack.

Due to the efforts of the breeder Samuel Handley of Manchester, this breed's name was adapted from Black and Tan to the Manchester Terrier.

MINIATURE SCHNAUZER
Terrier

Of the three Schnauzer breeds from Germany—Miniature, Standard, and Giant—the Miniature Schnauzer is the smallest. He originated from breeding with the Standard, the Affenpinscher, and the Brussels Griffon just before 1900, and now stands from twelve to fourteen inches at the shoulder. His weight is from ten to fifteen pounds.

The Miniature Schnauzer is always full of energy and is very devoted to his family. For his small size, he is a sturdy dog and has the resistance to withstand many more common canine ailments than other breeds of dogs.

His coat, like that of the other Schnauzers, is hard, wiry, and somewhat rough in appearance. He, also, is colored pepper and salt or similar mixtures, reddish pepper, pure black, or black and tan.

Due to the Miniature Schnauzer's love of home life, he is never one that roams and consequently makes an ideal companion dog.

Famous Miniature Schnauzer owners include Bill Cosby and Mary Tyler Moore.

According to the American Kennel Club, the Miniature Schnauzer is the most popular of the three Schnauzer breeds.

The Miniature Schnauzer's name is derived from the German word *Schnauze*, meaning "muzzle."

The Miniature Schnauzer is a bold dog, originally used for guarding small farms and families.

In Germany, these little dogs are called *Zwergschnauzer*.

NORWICH TERRIER
Terrier

The Norwich Terrier is twelve pounds in weight and ten inches high, an ideal size, set low to the ground. He was bred from an old English type of terrier and now suggests a small Irish Terrier, with his hard, wiry coat usually colored red. The Norwich Terrier may also include black and tan, reddish wheaten, and grizzle.

For what he may lack in beauty, the Norwich Terrier more than makes up with his fine disposition. He is a hardy dog for his size and is said to be a perfect demon, yet although he is full of spirit, he is not in the least quarrelsome.

The Norwich Terrier is an ancient English breed of strong constitution, tremendously active and with the ability to stand up and fight for his rights. In fact, judging standards for the breed emphasize that it is permissible for these dogs to have scars on their bodies, provided they are the result of honorable combat.

Originating in England, Norwich Terriers were purchased by students at Cambridge University to protect their dorm rooms from rats. They were eventually adopted as the university's mascot.

This breed has had many nicknames, such as the Cantab Terrier and the Trumpington Terrier, taking the name from the Cambridge street that was home to many university students. They are also known as the Jones Terrier, after breeder Frank Jones, who brought the first Norwich Terrier to the United States.

Referred to as one breed until 1964, the Norfolk Terrier and the Norwich Terrier have identifiable distinctions. The Norwich Terrier has erect and pointed ears, while the Norfolk Terrier's ears are dropped.

E.B. White had a Norwich Terrier named Jones.

A Norwich Terrier named Winky was a main character in Christopher Guest's movie *Best in Show*.

SCOTTISH TERRIER
Terrier

This low-slung terrier fits his name. He is typically a Scotsman and minds his own business, which is unlike most other terriers.

The Scottie is a useful breed. He is a good hunter of foxes, rats, and other small animals, and a good retriever for both land and water. His desire to be left alone by strangers makes him a good watchdog.

The Scottie stands only about ten inches high. His weight is from eighteen to twenty-two pounds. The coat of this alert little dog is short and very wiry, colored steel gray, brindle, sandy, or wheaten, with any white objectionable.

Rare dignity marks the Scottish Terrier as being an ideal dog for the modern home. He is a deep-loving breed and much prefers the companionship of his family to roaming. He is far from the type that demands attention, often choosing a quiet corner to snooze rather than excitement. The Scottie is a perfect gentleman at all times.

"Between 1929 and 1944, the Scottish Terrier was one of the most popular dogs in the world."

—*The Great Book of Dogs*

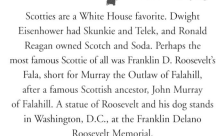

Scotties are a White House favorite. Dwight Eisenhower had Skunkie and Telek, and Ronald Reagan owned Scotch and Soda. Perhaps the most famous Scottie of all was Franklin D. Roosevelt's Fala, short for Murray the Outlaw of Falahill, after a famous Scottish ancestor, John Murray of Falahill. A statue of Roosevelt and his dog stands in Washington, D.C., at the Franklin Delano Roosevelt Memorial.

In *Lady and the Tramp*, Lady's trusty friend Jock is a Scottie—with an accent to prove it.

Humphrey Bogart, Joan Crawford, Bette Davis, Jacqueline Kennedy Onassis, and Charles Lindbergh all owned Scottish Terriers.

SEALYHAM TERRIER
Terrier

The low-built Sealyham Terrier from Wales is the result of probable breeding of the Dandie Dinmont Terrier and the Fox Terrier or the Bull Terrier. He is noted for his pluckiness in fighting game under the ground—a dog that is all courage, that knows how to fight.

In appearance, the Sealyham's body resembles that of the Dandie Dinmont, being built with curves rather than with the squareness of other terriers. His wiry coat is white and usually has some lemon or tan markings on the head and ears. His head appears to be large for his body, this aiding him greatly in his fighting.

He stands about ten inches high, and his weight is about twenty-three or twenty-four pounds.

The Sealyham Terrier is an intelligent little dog and learns new tricks or duties quickly. His good manners and even temperament, good size, and desire to do the master's bidding make him a splendid housedog.

Captain John Edwards developed the Sealyham Terrier at Sealy Ham in Wales, hence the breed's name.

Maurice Sendak had a Sealyham Terrier named Jennie, which was featured in his book *Higglety Pigglety Pop!*

"Originally the Sealyham's coat was reddish. Thus he was easily confused with the fox and got many of the bullets intended for it."
—*The Great Book of Dogs*

Not only did filmmaker Alfred Hitchcock cast himself in cameo appearances in his films, he also cast his Sealyham Terriers, Geoffrey and Stanley, which appeared in *The Birds* and *Suspicion*.

Other famous Sealyham owners include Humphrey Bogart, Richard Burton, Gary Cooper, Cary Grant, and Princess Margaret.

SKYE TERRIER
Terrier

The Isle of Skye, a part of Scotland, claims to be the origin of the Skye Terrier, where the breed was used for ferreting wildcats, badgers, foxes, martens, and other small animals from their hiding places in stone piles.

The Skye Terrier is distinguished by his coat, which is so long that his eyes and his feet can hardly be seen. The colors are blue, gray, or fawn with black tips. The weight of the Skye Terrier averages about twenty-five pounds; his height is nine to ten inches, his length measuring twice his height.

This capable hunter of ground animals is a plucky dog. He has even been used at times for hunting otter, one of the most ferocious water animals. His stubby legs and long coat dragging along the ground do not prevent the Skye Terrier from being lively. He is a curious little fellow, and though his eyes seem to be hidden from view, it is seldom that anything escapes his attention.

In 1858, a man named John Gray was buried in Greyfriar's churchyard in Edinburgh, Scotland. According to Scottish legend, Gray's devoted Skye Terrier, Bobby, slept upon his master's grave for the remaining fourteen years of his life. Greyfriar's Bobby—a statue immortalizing the little terrier— was erected at the site in his memory.

Skye Terriers have been nicknamed the Heavenly Breed.

"There was a time when any self-respecting duchess would have been ashamed to be seen in the park without her fashionable Skye Terrier."
—American Kennel Club

Queen Victoria was quite fond of her Skye Terriers, one of the many breeds of dogs that she owned.

STAFFORDSHIRE TERRIER
Terrier

This breed, popularly known as the Yankee Terrier and American Pit Bull Terrier, is one of the most capable dogs for his size. He is very stocky and muscular—a well put-together dog. He greatly resembles the Bull Terrier, on a smaller scale.

The Staffordshire Terrier, like the Bull Terrier, is noted for his ability as a fighting dog. He is an aggressive type and this, combined with his power, enables him to hold his own with other dogs, almost regardless of size. The Staffordshire Terrier is a dog of proverbial courage.

The Staffordshire Terrier varies in height from fourteen to sixteen inches. His weight is usually twenty-eight to thirty-eight pounds. Any color is permissible: Solid, parti-colored, or patches. The hair of the staff is rather stiff and short, lying close to the body.

The Staffordshire Terrier has the unique ability to instinctively distinguish between potentially threatening attackers and passive beings.

In the 1930s, Pete the Pup, a famous Staffordshire Terrier, starred in the original *Our Gang* comedies.

"In 1825, several [Staffordshire Terriers] were matched against a lion and showed no hesitation in going into the attack. Once they had tasted blood, they would fight to the death."

—Dogs

The American Staffordshire Terrier and the American Pit Bull Terrier were once a single breed but split into two in 1900, when dogfighting was banned in the United States. The former became the show strain, while the latter was labeled a fighting dog.

STANDARD SCHNAUZER
Terrier

The Standard Schnauzer, due to his handy size, ability as a watchdog, and desire to learn, has won a wide reputation for being an ideal house dog. Few breeds are more interested in their master's actions than this quiet dog from Germany.

The Standard Schnauzer is one of the three Schnauzer breeds, others including the Miniature and the Giant. He stands about eighteen inches high as compared with the Giant's twenty-four inches and the Miniature's twelve inches. All three of the Schnauzers have similar hard, wiry coats.

As a high-spirited dog, and at the same time one that is always reliable, the Standard Schnauzer excels. He is a great killer of vermin. He is easily trained in obedience, mostly because of his desire to please. The Standard Schnauzer is not interested in life other than that which is part of his own. He has little trace of that curiosity so apparent in many other breeds of dogs.

In German, this dog is called *Mittelschnauzer.*

Because of his loyal disposition and protective nature in watching over children, this dog has been nicknamed *Kinder Watcher* in Germany.

Thanks to its handsome and aristocratic bearing, this breed was a popular subject for artists Albrecht Dürer and Rembrandt.

Errol Flynn's Schnauzer Arno made his way around Hollywood, accompanying the actor to studios, nightclubs, and parties. Flynn once beat up a man for trying to harm his beloved dog.

During World War I, Standard Schnauzers were used as aides and dispatch carriers for the German army and the Red Cross.

WELSH TERRIER
Terrier

Cheerful, lively, loyal, courageous—these words best describe this member of the terrier clan from Wales. The Welsh Terrier is often referred to as a Miniature Airedale, though the two are definitely different breeds.

The Welsh Terrier is a very well-mannered dog. He loves children, does not tend toward being quarrelsome, and has a wonderfully even disposition entirely free of any viciousness. It is said that the Welsh Terrier is one of the least terrierlike breeds of the terrier family.

The coat of the Welsh Terrier is hard, wiry, and abundant, colored either black and tan or black, grizzle, and tan. Average height is fifteen inches; weight is about twenty pounds.

The Welsh Terrier is an excellent house dog. His size is ideal, and the fact that he is easygoing but a good watchdog and rat killer has given him a reputation for being a very intelligent dog.

A very young Caroline Kennedy was featured on the cover of *Woman's Day* magazine in 1962 with a Welsh Terrier named Charlie. Charlie belonged to her younger brother, John Jr., and was a gift from their grandfather, Joe Kennedy.

This breed is recognized as the oldest of his cousins, the Airedale and Irish Terriers.

The Welsh Terrier was known to assist hounds in hunting and is said to be an excellent hunter of fox, badger, and otter.

In the 1900s, this breed was also called the Black-and-Tan Wire Terrier and the Old English Terrier.

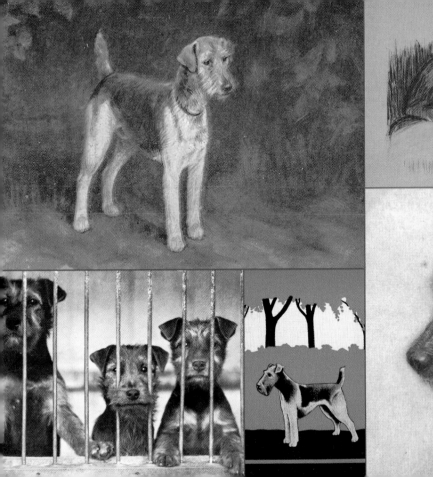

WEST HIGHLAND WHITE TERRIER
Terrier

The West Highland White Terrier could be mistaken for a white Scottish Terrier. He comes from Scotland and originated from blood closely related to the Scottish Terrier.

The Westie, as he is often affectionately called, is a merry and spunky little dog of excellent disposition. Though self-reliant, he is not one who roams, preferring to remain in his home beside his master. Always on his toes, he possesses a gameness and self-esteem found in few other breeds.

The West Highland White Terrier's rather long coat is always white in color and hard in texture, though he also has a furry undercoat. He weighs between thirteen and twenty-two pounds and measures from ten to twelve inches at the shoulder.

Outdoors, the West Highland White Terrier is a sporty, good hunter of endurance. He can keep up for hours under bad weather conditions and never whimper.

Legend has it that when a reddish type of terrier was mistakenly identified as a fox and shot during the hunt, Colonel Edward Malcolm, of Poltalloch, Scotland, was inspired to breed the West Highland White Terrier, which has a white coat that is clearly identifiable in the field. The breed was also called the Poltalloch Terrier.

Alfred Hitchcock had a Westie named Sarah, which notoriously slept on her own pillow snuggled between Mr. Hitchcock and his wife.

The West Highland White Terrier accompanies a Scottie as the logo for Black and White Scotch Whiskey.

In 1992, Jeff Koons created Puppy, a forty-three-foot-high topiary installation of a Westie, which included an irrigation system, twenty-five tons of soil, and more than 70,000 flowers. This colorful dog now resides at the Museo Guggenheim Bilbao.

AFFENPINSCHER
Toy

The Affenpinscher, often called the Monkey Terrier, is a native of Germany. He is a small dog but sturdy for one weighing less than eight pounds.

The coat of the Affenpinscher is an important factor from a judging standpoint. It is hard and wiry in texture, short and dense over certain parts of the body, and in other parts, shaggy and long.

The breed was first recognized in America in 1936, but he is a very old dog. Affenpinschers are generally quiet for toys. They can, however, become vehemently excited when they are attacked and are fearless toward any aggressor, large or small. This little monkey of the dog family is a thoroughly devoted pal to his master and home.

The most color for the Affenpinscher is black, though tan markings and mixtures of gray and red are permissible.

Known to be one of the oldest breeds of toy dogs, the Affenpinscher is believed to have originated in Germany in the 1600s.

These little dogs were known as excellent ratters and could often be found guarding farms or stores from vermin.

The Affenpinscher is nicknamed Monkey Dog, because of its monkeylike characteristics. It is believed to have derived its name from the German word *Affe,* meaning "monkey."

The French version of this nickname *Diablotin Moustachu*, which translates to "mustached little devil."

BRUSSELS GRIFFON

Toy

As the name implies, the little Brussels Griffon comes from Belgium. Several other toy breeds were likely used to originate him—namely, the Affenpinscher, the Pug, and the English Toy Spaniel. But this can only be assumption because the breed itself is many years old.

The Brussels Griffon's rough coat can be only reddish brown in color. This roughness, odd for a toy breed, added to his quaint facial expression, draws the attention of those passing him on the street or at shows.

This smaller breed of the Griffon family, which also includes the Wirehaired Pointing Griffon, is a hardy little fellow for a toy. He is rather distant to strangers but has an abundance of pep around his own family and furnishes many hours of amusement for those whom he selects for special attention.

Preferably, the Brussels Griffon should weigh between eight and ten pounds and should not weigh more than twelve pounds.

The "Brussels" in this breed's name refers to its provenance, Brussels, Belgium. The term "Griffon" comes from this dog's physical resemblance to the mythological griffin, "half eagle and half lion monster."

This breed is categorized into three varieties: the Brussels Griffon, the Belgian Griffon, and the Petit Barbançon.

In the early nineteenth century, it was customary for coachmen to keep these little dogs in their stables to control vermin.

Verdell—a main character in the 1997 film *As Good As It Gets*, with Jack Nicholson—was played by six different Brussels Griffons: Timer, Sprout, Debbie, Parfait, Billy, and Jill.

CHIHUAHUA
Toy

The Chihuahua originated in North America, coming from Mexico many years ago. This mite of a dog is the smallest in all dogdom. He weighs only one to six pounds and, although so tiny, makes an able watchdog by using his shrill bark. The Chihuahua is distinctive, with his apple-dome head and disproportionately large, erect ears. His facial expression is one of sauciness. He prefers his own kind and seldom has anything to do with other breeds.

There are two types of coats on the Chihuahua, the longhaired and the shorthaired. The coat may be any color, either solid or with markings of some different color.

He is a curious little dog, has a nice disposition, and is rather a modest sort until he becomes acquainted. When he does, he is ready for any kind of mischief. In spite of his size, the Chihuahua loves to hunt and finds vermin easily.

It was reported that Taco Bell spent more than $500 million on its memorable, "*Yo quiero* Taco Bell" campaign that featured its mascot Gidget, a Chihuahua.

Other famous Chihuahuas include Ren from the animated television series *The Ren and Stimpy Show*, Martini, belonging to Sharon Osbourne, and Bruiser, from the *Legally Blonde* films featuring Reese Witherspoon.

The Chihuahua is the smallest and the oldest breed in North America. According to the 2006 *Guinness Book of World Records*, a longhaired Chihuahua is the smallest living dog.

"Even the Chihuahua, named for its 'native' land—the state of Chihuahua in Mexico—is apparently the descendant of small Asiatic dogs and of long-coated ancient Mexican dogs called Techichi."
—*The Story of Dogs*

ENGLISH TOY SPANIEL
Toy

Records show the English Toy Spaniel to be the oldest of English toy breeds, having been known as far back as the first part of the sixteenth century. There are several varieties of this little dog, each of them rather well known. The black and tan strain is termed the King Charles Spaniel. Other strains are the Ruby Spaniel (chestnut red), the Prince Charles Spaniel (tri-colored black, white, and tan), and the Blenheim Spaniel (red and white).

This breed might be termed a toy Cocker Spaniel. He is rugged and robust for a toy dog and very much of a sporting dog in the field.

The English Toy Spaniel has a grand disposition, loves to live, and has proved to be a real pal.

Though he has lived in England for several centuries, there is little doubt that this perky little dog came from Asian countries, probably Japan, prior to his entrance to England.

Probably originating in Asia, English Toy Spaniels were likely given as gifts to English royalty.

It is said that one of Mary, Queen of Scots' beloved English Toy Spaniels was found by the Queen's executioner, hiding in the folds of her skirt.

Artists such as Titian, Anthony Van Dyck, Thomas Gainsborough, and Joshua Reynolds have featured English Toy Spaniels in paintings.

Dr. Caius, physician to Elizabeth I, described English Toy Spaniels as "comforters" and "gentle spaniels."

Varieties of this breed are nicknamed Charlie after King Charles II, who was very fond of these dogs. He declared that the breed be allowed in the House of Parliament, where they had formerly been prohibited.

ITALIAN GREYHOUND
Toy

This breed is the toy of the Greyhound family and derives his name from his former popularity in Italy. Like his larger cousins, the Italian Greyhound is hundreds of years old, and though of little working value, he is a splendid companion and offers many hours of enjoyment to his owners. He is an elegant little dog, exceptionally graceful in his free, high-stepping movement. No other breed is more docile than this little dog or more typically one of the toy dogs.

For the purpose of show-judging the breed, there are two weight classes—one for under eight pounds and one for more than eight pounds. The smaller the dog, the more desirable he is.

From the tip of his very slender muzzle to the tip of his fine tail, the Italian Greyhound is tiny. His coat has a satiny gloss and may be colored fawn, red, mouse, blue, cream, or white, while a black and tan combination is not permissible.

The delicate Italian Greyhound is the smallest of the sight hounds.

One of these little dogs was discovered mummified in the lava remains at Pompeii.

Italian Greyhounds have been very popular with royalty. Royal owners include Queen Anne, Queen Victoria, Catherine the Great, Frederick the Great, and Queen Maud of Norway.

An elegant and fashionable breed, the Italian Greyhound was frequently the subject of Renaissance paintings, such as Gerard David's *The Virgin and Child with Saints*.

Though both breeds resemble small Greyhounds, the Italian Greyhound is one third the size of a Whippet, and a much more delicate dog.

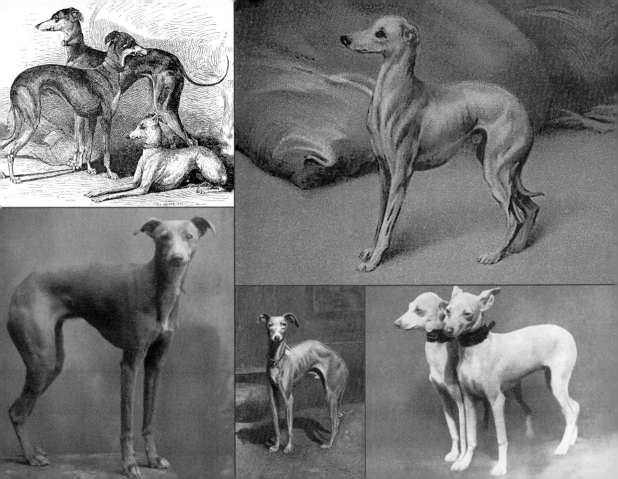

JAPANESE CHIN
Toy

This very old toy breed had a history closely linked with Japanese royalty and worship, though it is generally believed that the breed started in China. Oddly, years ago these little dogs were kept in cages, the way a canary is kept. They are dainty dogs and are often confused with the English Toy Spaniel.

The Japanese Chin is a member of the Far Eastern canine family, which includes the Pug and the Pekingese. The profuse and silky coat of this toy resembles to some extent that of the Pekingese. He is a parti-colored dog, being either black and white or red and white. Height varies from eight to eleven inches; weight, between four and fifteen pounds.

The Japanese Chin is a lively little dog of high-breeding and style. He lifts his legs high as he trots along and carries his heavily feathered tail proudly over his back. He is sensitive, and his feelings are easily hurt. He never loves unless that love is thorough and lifelong.

The Japanese Spaniel became officially known as the Japanese Chin in 1977.

This breed was given as a gift to Queen Victoria from Commodore Perry upon his return from Japan in 1853, but it was her daughter-in-law, Princess Alexandra, who collected Japanese Chins, eventually owning twenty-six. Her favorites were named Facey and Little Marvel.

Japanese Chins were the desired lapdog of aristocracy, exclusively owned by the emperors of Japan and members of the Imperial family. They were never to belong to commoners.

The white spot on the Japanese Chin's forehead is called a Buddha's thumbprint because Emperor Ming Ti claimed that Buddha touched these little dogs.

Famous Japanese Chin owners include Deborah Harry of Blondie and the Osbournes.

MALTESE
Toy

As the name implies, the Maltese comes from the island of Malta, located in the Mediterranean Sea. He is the most ancient of toy breeds, having been a great favorite as a lapdog of women in Greece and Rome. Aristotle made mention of the Maltese in some of his writings.

The breed is a sporty one, fearless even so far as attacking vermin equaling him in size. The Maltese is tiny. Preferably, dogs should weigh between four and six pounds and not exceed seven pounds. The coat is all white, long, straight, and silky; in fact, it is so long that it drags along the ground when he walks.

The Maltese is smart, affectionate, and quite like a Toy Spaniel. He is a hardy little fellow, considering that for more than twenty-eight centuries, he has been coddled to death and treated as a doll. Often called the aristocrat of the animal world, he has been petted by ladies of royalty and is truly a high-bred dog.

The Greeks paid homage to their Maltese by erecting tombs for them.

Elizabeth Taylor had a beloved Maltese named Sugar, which accompanied the actress to award shows and social events. After Sugar died in 2005, Taylor got a new Maltese, Daisy.

Publis, the Roman governor of Malta, cherished his Maltese, Issa, so much that he commissioned a portrait of his beloved dog.

"Many people long ago thought that they could put the little dogs right next to them at the end of their beds when they were ill, and the Maltese would have healing and comforting qualities."
—Westminster Kennel Club

Tallulah Bankhead had a Maltese named Doloras.

MINIATURE PINSCHER
Toy

The Miniature Pinscher is called a Toy Doberman almost as frequently as he is called a Miniature Pinscher. This high-stepping little dog has most of the physical qualities of the Doberman Pinscher, on a smaller scale.

For a toy breed weighing but eight to ten pounds and standing roughly ten to twelve inches in height, this perky dog is quite sturdy. He is a great show-off, always wanting to attract attention, and is a splendid watchdog for his size.

The color of the Miniature Pinscher can be black with tan markings like the Doberman, solid yellow, stag red, dark blue, or brown with red markings. The coat is rather hard for a toy, with straight, short, and very shiny hair. He is an attractive little fellow in both appearance and personality.

The Miniature Pinscher was bred in Germany, where it is called a *Zwergpinscher*. In German, *Zwerg* means "midget" or "dwarf."

There are two distinct nicknames for the Miniature Pinscher: Minpin, as it is called by enthusiasts, and *Reh*, meaning "doe" in German.

While the Miniature Pinscher looks like the Doberman, they are not at all related.

Lucky Luciano, the famous Mafia boss, owned a Miniature Pinscher, appropriately named Mafia.

This dog is also known as the King of Toys because of his attention-grabbing style and personality.

Miniature Pinschers have a specific gait similar to that of Hackney ponies; they lift their legs high when they walk, with a definite bend at the wrist.

PAPILLON
Toy

The Papillon is a French toy dog with a kindly disposition suggested by the French meaning of the breed name, which is "butterfly." It is probable that the Papillon originated from other toy spaniels and the longhaired Chihuahua, which he seems to resemble more closely than any other breed.

He is a graceful little dog with attractive pure colors of white with black, orange, tan, or brown markings. Papillons are famed as the favorite pets of such regal ladies as Marie Antoinette and Madame de Pompadour. They are very clean-living dogs and, though dainty in their movements, are surprisingly hardy. They weigh less than ten pounds and are eight to eleven inches high.

The Papillon, with his pleasing personality and his ability to adapt himself quickly to many kinds of different living conditions, is one of the best little pets in dogdom.

The Papillon's name is the French word for "butterfly," as his large, fluttery ears look like butterfly wings and the blaze on his forehead brings to mind the body of the butterfly.

The drop-eared version of the Papillon is called the Phalene, which means "moth" in French.

Marie Antoinette is believed to have carried a Papillon in her arms on her way to the guillotine in 1793. The pup was spared and taken to a building that is still referred to today as the Papillon House.

In the eighteenth century, the Papillon was quite popular in France and often appeared in paintings by Jean-Honoré Fragonard, Peter Paul Reubens, and Anthony Van Dyck.

Madame de Pompadour had two Papillons named Inez and Mimi.

PEKINGESE
Toy

This sturdy, long-lived little dog is the royal dog of China, having been accurately bred for centuries in that country by royal families. This has perhaps made him the dignified dog he is today. He is truly an aristocratic breed in spite of his small stature.

The Pekingese has at different times during his existence been called lion dog for his lionlike appearance; Sun Dog for his beautiful golden-red coat so long and straight; and Sleeve Dog, for he was formerly carried in the huge sleeves of the robes worn by the members of the Imperial household in China.

The Pekingese is quite an independent dog for his size, which must not exceed fourteen pounds, though he is a cuddly little toy and adores the love of his owner. The Pekingese may be of almost any color, but the above-mentioned red is the one most commonly seen.

❧

The Pekingese can be traced back to the Tang Dynasty and was regarded as a manifestation of the legendary foo dog that drove away spirits. If an emperor died, his Pekingese were sacrificed so they could protect him in the afterlife. Commoners had to bow to these little dogs of nobility, and anyone who stole one was sentenced to death.

❧

Walt Disney's animated Pekingese, Fifi the Peke, was Minnie Mouse's dog and Pluto's girlfriend.

❧

The five Pekingese that survived when British and French troops overran the Summer Palace during the Second Opium War were taken to Queen Victoria. She appropriately named one Looty. It is from these canine spoils of war that the modern Pekingese is descended.

❧

Shirley Temple had a Pekingese named Ching-Ching II.

POMERANIAN
Toy

Few breeds are as furry as the Pomeranian. His coat is a mass of fluff, which would cause him to look almost like a little ball were it not for the break made by his foxlike head. The Pom comes in many different colors from black to white, including parti-colors. He is a toy in size, generally weighing from three to seven pounds.

The Pomeranian owes his development to breeders in the small province of Pomerania, located in the northeastern part of Germany. It is probable that these fanciers bred the Pomeranian down to his present size from the old Wolf Spitz, whose ancestors were Iceland Sledge Dogs.

The Pom is truly a vivacious breed. He makes an adorable companion combining boldness in action and docility in temper. This, plus his keen sense of hearing, makes him one of the best watchdogs among the small breeds. He learns tricks easily and is always desirous of pleasing his mistress.

Two of the three dogs that survived the *Titanic* were Pomeranians. One belonged to Margaret Hays and the other to Mrs. Elizabeth Barrett Rothschild.

It is believed that while Michelangelo painted the Sistine Chapel, his Pomeranian kept him company by sitting on a satin pillow nearby.

Mozart had a Pomeranian named Pimperl to which he dedicated an aria. And Chopin was so enamored of his girlfriend's Pomeranian that he composed the "Valse des Petits Chiens."

Diamond, Sir Isaac Newton's Pomeranian, was believed to have caused his nervous breakdown by tipping over a candle, which set Sir Isaac's manuscripts containing more than twenty years of research afire.

While on her deathbed, Queen Victoria is reported to have demanded that her favorite Pomeranian, Turi, be delivered to her.

PUG
Toy

The Pug, very popular during the 1890s, is large for a toy breed, some specimens weighing as much as eighteen pounds. He is also among the hardiest of toys, his muscular body giving him the appearance of a powerful dog. He is really a toy in name only.

Though called the Dutch Dog, the Pug is probably Chinese. This nickname was given to him as a result of his great popularity in Holland. He is one of the cleanest of all dogs, making a splendid house pet due to his cleanliness, and he decides many problems for himself.

The coat of the Pug is fine and smooth, and has rather a glossy texture. Colors are silver fawn, apricot fawn, or black, with a black mask easily distinguishable on his face.

The Pug is a useful breed, being a good killer of rats and chaser of rabbits, in addition to his well-known ability to guard his domicile intelligently. Few breeds are more self-reliant than the tidy little Pug.

"Ladies of the eighteenth and nineteenth centuries liked to keep Pugs, convinced that against the dog's ugliness, their own beauty would stand out."

—*The Great Book of Dogs*

When her husband, Napoleon, was in jail, Josephine Bonaparte sent secret notes to him, concealing the messages in her Pug Fortune's collar.

The Duke and Duchess of Windsor had more than eleven Pugs, which traveled with them everywhere. Personal chefs attended to the dogs' every need, including spraying them with Miss Dior, the Duchess's favorite perfume.

Movie-star pugs include Otis from the film *The Adventures of Milo and Otis*, and Frank, the canine star of *Men in Black.*

Fashion designer Valentino owns five Pugs: Molly, Margo, Monty, Milton, and Maude.

TOY MANCHESTER TERRIER
Toy

Another member of the black-and-tan family of dogdom is the Toy Manchester Terrier, a diminutive phase of the Manchester Terrier, ideally weighing between six and seven pounds, but should not exceed twelve pounds. He is also called the Toy Black-and-Tan Terrier.

This little dog with the coloring of the Doberman Pinscher is one of the most alert and active of all dogs. As he struts, his lengthy legs of pencil-thin proportions attract much attention.

He possesses a strong personality, is smart, and, in spite of his toy size, is quite hardy. His short, glossy coat, small size, and love of his own family make the Toy Manchester Terrier a splendid dog for the small house or apartment. He is a good watchdog, giving alarm to intrusions by shrill barking. Surprisingly, the Toy Manchester is a good killer of vermin, and he will courageously go after a rat his size and even larger, stopping only after his job is finished.

"Until 1959, the Manchester Terrier and Toy Manchester were registered as separate breeds although inter-breeding was permitted. Since then, the two breeds have combined to form one breed, the Manchester Terrier, with two varieties: Toy and Standard."
—American Kennel Club

It is reported that Toy Manchester Terriers were referred to as Grooms' Pocket Pieces, since they were often carried in custom leather pouches that attached to a horseman's belt.

This breed has also been called the Gentleman's Terrier.

In 1848, a Toy Manchester Terrier named Tiny killed three hundred rats in fifty-four minutes and fifty-four seconds.

TOY POODLE
Toy

The Toy Poodle is an elegant little dog that shows intelligence in his almost human facial expression. He was bred down from the larger Poodle and, in all probability, from the early dog of Malta. The Toy Poodle weighs between six and nine pounds and stands up to ten inches high, while the Miniature Poodle variety weighs between fifteen and seventeen pounds and stands between ten and fifteen inches in height. Like his cousins, the Toy Poodle may be any solid color and has the same curly or corded coat as they have.

It is interesting to note that the Toy Poodle is the principal ancestor of England's truffle dog, which was used to go underground to scent this delicacy. The Toy Poodle has great scenting powers, and this, added to his sagacity, made him an ideal dog to combine with the digging terrier in forming the valuable truffle dog.

The Toy Poodle has all the instincts for hunting and ratting of his bigger cousins and is a fine house dog—proud, well built, and smart. He learns much for himself and can be taught tricks easily.

Jacqueline Susann's bestselling novel *Every Night, Josephine* was written about her beloved Poodle.

After divorcing Arthur Miller, Marilyn Monroe received a Poodle from Frank Sinatra, which she named Maf due to Sinatra's alleged Mafia connections. The dog was rumored to sleep on a fur coat given to her by her ex-husband.

The German word for Poodle is *Puddelhund*, while in France, Portugal, and Spain, the breed is known as *Caniche*.

Liberace owned a Toy Poodle named Suzette.

YORKSHIRE TERRIER

Toy

The Yorkshire Terrier's beauty lies in his silky coat parted down his back and reaching to the ground. The body coat is a steel blue, while the legs and head are a rich golden tan. The dog carries himself with a proud, important air, seeming to realize that he is a beautiful little dog.

It is believed that much Skye Terrier blood is present in the Yorkshire Terrier, though he also has some relation to the Maltese, the Dandie Dinmont Terrier, and other terriers. He weighs only about five pounds.

The Yorkshire Terrier from England is an active and spirited toy, always ready for play and attention. So much so, in fact, that it is often necessary to restrain his antics if his long, flowing coat is not to become spoiled. Were it not for his tiny size, the Yorkshire Terrier could be considered all terrier, for he owns all the natural characteristics of the numerous members of dogdom's terrier clan.

The Yorkshire Terrier is often seen adorned with a ribbon tying his hair up above his eyes. This is not just for show; it is to keep the Yorkie's face and food clear of hair.

Audrey Hepburn owned a Yorkshire Terrier named Mr. Famous, which was tragically hit by a car. She was given a replacement Yorkie named Assam of Assam by her husband, Mel Ferrer.

Smokey, the World War II pet of William Wynne, accompanied him on 150 air raids and twelve air-sea rescue missions, entertained the troops with her tricks, and assisted the Signal Corps by carrying a telegraph wire through a seventy-foot pipe.

According to the 2002 *Guinness Book of World Records*, the smallest dog ever recorded was a Yorkshire Terrier named Big Boss, which stood 4.7 inches tall.

THE MIXED BREEDS

The original edition of *The Red Book of Dogs* did not include a section on mixed-breed dogs, probably because it is their purebred relatives that take center stage in competition and the public eye. Nevertheless, these dogs—bred from any assortment of pure breeds or mutts themselves—are just as adorable, loyal, and full of personality as their pedigree cousins.

Unfortunately, so many of these mixed-breed dogs are abandoned or given to animal shelters, but if they are lucky enough to find an owner, they too will become loyal companions and friends.

Recently, there has been a controversial trend in the dog world regarding the introduction of "dog hybrids" or "designer dogs" such as the Puggle (Pug-Beagle mix) and the Labradoodle (Labrador Retriever-Poodle mix). While the verdict is still out about the future of these deliberately mixed breeds, one thing is certain. Regardless of their ancestry or lack of pedigree, throughout history, the mixed-breed dog has always been an important member of the canine race, especially to those who have owned or loved one.

Because of their ancestral backgrounds, which often consist a mixture of several pure breeds, mixed-breed dogs are sometimes called Heinz 57s.

Benji—perhaps the most famous mixed-breed dog in movie history—was originally played by a mutt named Higgins at the ripe old age of fourteen.

A mutt named Fido belonging to President Abraham Lincoln was the first presidential dog to ever have his photo taken.

"My dog is half Pit Bull, half Poodle. Not much of a watchdog, but a vicious gossip."

—comedian Craig Shoemaker

The popular canine star of the television series *Mad About You* was a mixed breed named Murray.

In the southern United States, a small mixed-breed dog is called a Feist or a Fice.

LIST OF BREEDS

Affenpinscher
Afghan Hound
Airedale Terrier
Basset Hound
Beagle
Bedlington Terrier
Bloodhound
Border Terrier
Borzoi
Brussels Griffon
Bullterrier, Colored Variety
Bullterrier, White Variety
Cairn Terrier
Chihuahua
Dachshund, Longhaired
Dachshund, Smooth
Dachshund, Wirehaired
Dandie Dinmont Terrier
English Toy Spaniel

Foxhound, American
Foxhound, English
Fox Terrier, Smooth-Haired Variety
Fox Terrier, Wirehaired Variety
Greyhound
Harrier
Irish Terrier
Italian Greyhound
Irish Wolfhound
Japanese Chin
Kerry Blue Terrier
Lakeland Terrier
Lhasa Apso
Maltese
Manchester Terrier
Miniature Pinscher
Miniature Schnauzer
Norwegian Elkhound
Norwich Terrier

Otterhound
Papillon
Pekingese
Pomeranian
Pug
Saluki
Scottish Deerhound
Scottish Terrier
Sealyham Terrier
Skye Terrier
Staffordshire Terrier
Standard Schnauzer
Toy Manchester Terrier
Toy Poodle
Welsh Terrier
West Highland White Terrier
Whippet
Yorkshire Terrier

BIBLIOGRAPHY

Albin, Dickie, et al., *The Dog*. New York: Exeter Books, 1982.

Big Dogs Little Dogs, the World of Our Canine Companions. A&E. New York: GT Publishing Corporation, 1998.

Borrer, Wendy, John Holmes, Margaret Osborne, Mary Roslin-Williams, Alan Hitchens, and Howar Loxton. *The Love of Dogs*. London: Octopus Books Limited, 1974.

Cobb, Bert. *Hunting Dogs*. New York: The Crafton Collection, Inc., 1931.

———. *Portraits of Dogs*. New York: The Crafton Collection, Inc., 1931.

The Complete Dog Book, 20th Edition. Official Publication of the American Kennel Club. New York: Ballantine Books, 2006.

Cook, Gladys Emerson. *American Champions*. New York: The Macmillan Company, 1945.

Dawson Lucy. *Dogs As I See Them*. New York: Grosset & Dunlap, 1937.

———. *Dogs Rough and Smooth*. New York: Grosset & Dunlap, 1936.

Dawson, Major A.J. *Everybody's Dog Book*. Illustrations by Thomas Fall. London: Philip Allan, 1922.

———. *Everybody's Dog Book*. New York: Frederick A. Stokes Company, 1922.

Dennis, Morgan. *The Morgan Dennis Dog Book (with Some Special Cats)*. New York: The Viking Press, 1946.

Dudman, Helga. *The Dog's Guide to Famous Owners*. Great Britain: Robson Books Ltd. 1997.

Hutchinson's Popular and Illustrated Dog Encyclopaedia. Edited by Walter Hutchinson. London: Hutchinson & Co. Ltd., 1935.

Lawson, James Gilchrist. *The Book of Dogs*.
Chicago: Rand McNally & Company, 1934.

Mery, Ferdinand. *The Life, History and Magic of the Dog*.
London: Cassell & Company Ltd., 1968.

Pugnetti, Gino. *The Great Book of Dogs: An International Anthology*. New York: Galahad Books, 1973.

Shuttlesworth, Dorothy. *The Story of Dogs*.
Garden City, N.Y.: Doubleday & Co. Inc., 1961.

Terhune, Albert Payson. *Real Tales of Real Dogs*.
Akron, Ohio: Saalfield Publishing Company, 1935.

Thorne, Diana. *Your Dogs and Mine*.
New York: Loring & Mussey, 1935.

WEB REFERENCES

akc.org
bond.senate.org
british-manchester-terrier-club.co.uk
chinpuppies.com
dogbreedinfo.com
dog-names.org
ebay.com
edinburougharchitecture.com
eisenhower.archives.gov
faqs.org
filmsite.org
hsus.org
irishfieldsports.com
littlepaws.com
marilynfan.org
martycrisp.com
nationalgeographic.com
olive-drab.com
petnet.com
thebreedsofdogs.com
titanic.com
westminsterkennelclub.org
wikipedia.com

And all of the individual dog-breed/club websites.

ACKNOWLEDGMENTS

I WOULD LIKE TO EXTEND A VERY SPECIAL THANK YOU TO THE FOLLOWING:

The American Kennel Club for the use of their archive collection, specifically **Megan Lyons** and **Kira Sexton**, for their help with collecting the many images from the archive.

My assistant and dear friend, **Daphne Birch**, for diligently helping to organize the insurmountable array of images and information in this book.

Art director and designer, **Ilana Anger** and **Agnieszka Stachowicz**, for elegantly capturing all the wonderful dogs in this book's bright and whimsical design.

Dinah Fried, the most efficient, hardworking, and pleasant editor one could ever have.

And senior editor, **Elizabeth Viscott Sullivan**, for her extraordinary love of dogs, especially Otis and Lulu, and her amazing ability to continue to raise the bar in her quest for excellence.